I Married My

Best Friend

Terry Bams

TABLE OF CONTENTS

<u>Note To Men</u>

Note To Women

Why your relationship with God is important

How to get your man on the same page when it comes to God

What's your purpose

When the relationship is going through a storm, how to get God involved

How to learn when it's best to listen and not talk

The importance of communication

How to communicate with a man

How to get through to him, when he won't say a word

When trust is lost, how to rebuild it

How to get over the hump of infidelity

How to let go and move forward

What is the root of trust

What you should do when value is lost

How to know when it's time to let go

Acknowledgements

First and foremost, I want to thank God. Without Him, there would be no book, no me and no anything. I want to thank my supporters. You are the other half of the reason that I wrote this book. I truly feel that if everyone could treat their partner like they do their best friend, the world would be a better place, so now I have put this advice into a book format, to show all how to get to that point.

I want to thank my wife for blessing the cover with me. I didn't think you would do it, but girl you know you FINE!

I'm blessed that God has given me the wisdom to now have something that will outlive me and help millions of people until the end of time. It makes my heart smile every time someone tells me how I've helped them through a dark time in their relationship or just life and God gets all the Glory!

Last, no matter what happens in life, always remember that there is only failure in us, and not God! When you are lost, turn to Him and He will always show you the way.

ISBN-13: 978-1483993867

Introduction

Relationships can be challenging. This is an understatement, however, since in the 21st century, statistics demonstrate that married couples are more likely to get divorced before reaching five years of marriage than surpassing it. So, what is the solution? Not many in our society have focused on the promotion of creating and sustaining the healthy relationship of couples rather than exploiting their demise.

As a self-proclaimed former womanizer, author and relationship coach, I, Terry Bams, will meet this challenge here. The experiences of my past have motivated me to share my present and future, beneficial relationship that I have built with my wife and God who has given me wisdom. Through my wife, I have found a friend. Over years of friendship, we became best friends. I have found friendship to be the key of sustenance for couples. However, this is not always easy. It calls for individuals to let go of self and be a willing, functioning half that makes a whole through the union with another that has also become selfless in part.

My efforts here will attempt to enlighten you on the importance of establishing a spiritual connection with God. In turn, you allow yourself to be more open to sharing your life with someone special.

Here lies the solution to maintaining a healthy marriage, partnership, dating relationship, and friendship. The chapters within this book have specific guidelines for men and women. Review your designated sections accordingly.

Lastly, be encouraged to now explore and investigate the possibilities in a new outlook on relationships, God, and the love needed for both.

1. A Man's Relationship with God

Without God, a relationship is nothing.

There is no such thing as a perfect relationship, but we do serve a perfect God. The key element in a relationship is commitment. We often say that we have a relationship with God, but still lack commitment. Marriage requires commitment and all relationships require commitment.

Commitment consists of spending time together, investing happiness and joy within the relationship, remaining faithful, being honest, trustworthy, and working to stay committed through the good and the bad. God needs the same commitment.

Why your relationship with God is important to the relationship. Everything that you want in your relationship or marriage will only be fulfilled through your commitment. You would not be happy with your woman, if she only came home 3 nights a week. You would want her there every day and night. Having a part-time woman is not a commitment. Moreover, if you do not attend church, pray, or active in your church and being the example that God made you to be, you are not having a committed relationship with Him. There is no failure in God, but only in us. Your success with your relationship is a result of your commitment to God. That is why it is important to make sure your relationship with Him is intact.

Most men think or believe marriage is just a piece of paper, another tax bracket, more headaches and confusion. The funny thing is, years ago, I had felt the same way until I received the truth.

He who finds a wife finds a good thing and receives favor from the Lord. ~ Proverbs 18:22

Two are better than one, because they have a good return for their work. If one falls down, his mate can help him up. But pity the man who falls and has no one to help him up! ~ **Ecclesiastes 4:9**

Then the Lord God said, "It is not good for the man to be alone." ~ **Genesis 2:18**

A man leaves his father and mother and bonds with his wife and they become one flesh. ~ **Genesis 2:24**

What's your purpose in the relationship. God purposed men to have favor and receive blessings when he finds a wife. When He gave Adam his Eve, she was a gift, a blessing, a helpmate, and the missing link that God knew Adam would need to fulfill His purpose.

Since we were born of sin and we have our imperfections, you will experience short comings and make mistakes within your relationship with

God. For example, when Eve was deceived, she ate the fruit. It was a gift and a curse. She was blessed with the gift to reproduce life and the curse of having to deal with the pains in bearing children. Moreover, there is no way the world would have multiplied with more humans without her mistake. Therefore, you will not be perfect. You will make mistakes, but you will need to learn from them and allow them to make you better. With every cause, there is an effect. Eve's effect from eating the fruit was that God ordered her to become submissive to her husband and Adam was to rule over her. It was Eve who was deceived and not Adam, and that suggests that God trusts you as the man to lead His kingdom according to His word and not follow the world.

DO – *Be the head of the household in your home as God purposed you to be*. *Just like Adam, you must lead so that your wife can follow. Take your family to bible study and church every Sunday and* *lead in prayer each night. Your woman should not have a problem submitting to you as long as you follow the word of God. Be led by the word of God, and not of the world. If you are not married and are just in a relationship, you should still practice going to bible study and church together and you both can pray every night, even if it is over the phone or on Skype. Don't wait to put God first when you get married, keep Him first all of the time. Do this even before the day you say, "I do." Join a ministry, whether it is the choir or the usher board. You need to remain connected at all times, so the foundation of your home never gets destroyed when troubles come. You need to be the example for your family in order to show the works of God. He made you in His own image and it is time for you to commit.*

DO - *Listen to Gospel music 100% of your day*. *The music we listen to plants seeds in our mind and* *affects our feelings. It is a root to our spirit. This method will have your ears hearing encouraging music and positive spirits. The anointing in the music will move your spirit in the right direction. In return, what your ears are hearing, your mind will start thinking differently and your emotions will start to change for the better. Next, stop watching all the negative things on TV including, reality shows, drama-filled movies and music videos. Your mind has to go through a transformation stage and to whom much is given, much is required. Sacrifice is the key, if you want your situation to change. The devil is always busy and you will not be perfect, but as long as you use these methods, you will be able to stay focused.*

It is important as a man that you lead and not dictate. For example, your woman may do the laundry, wash the dishes and clean all of the time. But, just like us, she is human and faced with some of the same issues we have as men. She gets tired, forgets things and wants a break at times. It will not kill you to wash a dish every once and a while, vacuum the carpet or just help out in other ways. Think on this. If you were single, you would have to do it yourself, anyway, so let's start leading and not dictating.

Husbands, love your wives, just as Christ loved the church and gave Himself up for her. ~ Ephesians 5:25

In this same way, husbands ought to love their wives as their own bodies. He who loves his wife loves himself. After all, no one ever hated his own body, but he feeds and cares for it, just as Christ does the church. ~ Ephesians 5:28

DON'T - Use the word of God when it only benefits you and you just want to have your way. For example: "She needs to be submissive to me; obey and listen to me no matter how crazy my mind is." That is false; women know when you are being led by the spirit or by the world. The word of God is not just meant for your benefit. It is designed for the benefit of men and women. If you are only her boyfriend, do not expect for her to be submissive. Her body only becomes yours when she becomes your wife. I do understand you have to "date" to become husband and wife, but if she is giving you the cow, why work for the milk? Learn to work for the milk when you are dating a woman that you may seek as a wife and life partner.

How to maintain your relationship with God in the midst of your storm. A God-fearing woman will submit to a God-fearing man. Your relationship with God builds the foundation of the relationship with your woman. You are the example for your family. Marriage is a vow you take before God. Marriage is not about the piece of paper, the wedding, the rings and not what the world made it to be. Those vows you take join two flesh, and make a union of one. It also takes a house and makes it a home. It sets the example for your children and grandchildren. If you can bow before God as a man, you will be able to stand up for anything.

Submit yourselves, then, to God. Resist the devil, and he will flee from you. Come near to God and he will come near to you. ~ James 4:7-8

-Submitting yourselves one to another in the fear of God ~ Ephesians 5:21

Most relationships and marriages do not work out because the foundation of the home is not built correctly. God provides the stones, bricks, sliding and mold for the home to stay together. Even if your wife or girlfriend seeks God, it is your responsibility as the man to lead, seek, understand and apply his principles to your family. If God wanted women to do it, He would have created Adam for Eve and have Eve to lead mankind. If your relationship is falling apart, take a look in the mirror. Ask yourself, "Do I truly have a relationship with God? Am I 100% committed to Christ? Am I taking my family to church on Sundays and to bible study? Am I truly submitting to God or am I just trying to trust that I can make it on my own?" God does not forsake the righteous, so if the answer to all those questions is not YES, you need to adjust your life and get your relationship back right with God. Remember "He who finds a wife, finds a good thing and receive favor from the Lord" (Proverbs). God does not go back on His word. When He says it, it is done!

2. A Man's Communication

A fool finds no pleasure in understanding, but delights in airing his own opinions. ~ Proverbs 18:2

As a man, communication seems to always be a challenge. It is said that "The best communicator is the one whom listens the best." We also know in relationships, women will always do most of the talking. We, as men, need to do most of the listening. Men, you must start looking at this as a positive, and not a negative. Take a step back and let's walk down memory lane.

The importance of communication. Remember the first, second or even the third time that you went to a car lot to purchase a car. As soon as you pulled up and walked out of your car, was the salesman there to greet you with a smile? In your head and many car shoppers' minds, a car salesman is the last person we would like to deal with, but we have no choice because we want to buy a car. The key thing to a car sale is him listening. He needs to find out what you are interested in and not interested in. If you wanted a 4x4 truck, he would not show you a sports car or if you wanted a four door nice sedan, he would not show you a van. He would not for several reasons. 1. He would not want to look stupid. 2. You would look at him wondering, "Are you listening to me?" 3. He would not sell you a car and collect his commission. Salesman would rather you buy the car, house or just a cell phone. For this, they become the best listeners in the world to provide you with what you need. Do not worry men; we are not done walking down memory lane.

Remember when you met your woman and went out on that first date? I know you are having that blank stare right now, but that moment will catch up with you. The first date was all you had to get you to the point of her becoming your wife, girlfriend or even getting past that first encounter. The most important action that you did on that date was listening. You listened to her talk about the cat you have grown to love, her talking about her best friend that you still do not like, her favorite color that she seems to think looks good on you also, and everything it would take for you to get a second date. No matter what happened on that first date, you had to listen, understand, and then speak in order for the communication to work between you two.

He who answers before listening, that is his foolishness and his shame. ~ Proverbs 18:13

Everyone should be quick to listen, slow to speak and slow to become angry. ~ James 1:19

How to defeat the nagging. Currently in your relationship if her talking sounds like nagging, well believe there is some truth in that nag, and you failed at just listening. Most women nag in the sense of trying to fix the issue before it turns into a big problem.

DON'T - *Talk at this point; just listen. Getting upset or having an attitude does not put out the fire. Water does. Water is love and listening at this point provides you with understanding. As she talks, do not make excuses, listen and correct the faults. These steps do not make you less of a man; it creates an environment where you can lead by example. If you can listen, understand and apply, then in return, she will do the same.*

At times in the relationship, the two of you will not see eye to eye, but communication is the **MOST IMPORTANT THING IN THE RELATIONSHIP**. Think about it for a second. When she is mad and you two are not talking, it does not lead to sex, happiness and joy. As the man, you have to be the bigger person most of the time. Even when you feel you are not wrong, you need to talk to your woman. The answer is not leaving outside the house, talking to your friends, family or another woman. The issue is with the woman in your home. If you find the both of you arguing and fighting in the house a lot and it seems like you can never talk there, find somewhere new to just talk. Do something different in order to have a different result.

DO – *Both of you need to pick 2-3 days out of the week to talk for 1 hour minimum for 90 days OUTSIDE OF THE HOUSE. Most fights and confusion occur in the house. So you need to change the environment; talking in a negative environment always just plants that negative spirit or feeling back within your mind and body. The first day, talk about the first time you all met, the first date, the first time you fell in love with each other and the first time that you realized that you wanted to be in a relationship. This talk is important because it takes you back down memory lane to remind yourself why you are still together. The other days, you need to talk about anything, and everything, but nothing negative. This will build understanding, value and a strong communication base in the relationship. Even if you two have been together for years; everyday you will still learn something new.*

Next you need to always say something positive before you address any situation. When you come right out of the gate with something negative on top of a negative situation, it just leaves it to be more negative than it was before. For example: "Baby I love you........." "We've been having a lot of great days....." "I'm glad you're in my life....." This method defuses the tension before it even happens. When it is nice outside, take your lady for a walk in the park and talk. Nice weather, nice scenery always creates great positive feelings.

If you want different results, you must start today and do things different.

What to say, and what you should avoid saying. Since we are on the topic of talking, men you need to do a lot more of it. Women are not mind readers or psychics. If you married her or agreed to be in a relationship, you owe it to yourself to let her hear your voice. Not in the sense of talking at her, but with her. I know you are thinking, "Terry, what do you mean?" Do not worry because I will explain. As a man, it is in our essence to be hard, tough, and rough and not show our sensitive side. Guess what? For your woman, it is time that you do. It makes the relationship go so much easier, and she will understand that you too have feelings. It is your job to lead by example and not dictate. Everything starts and ends with you. Even though you might make her seem like she is in control, she should know just how far she can push that control. When God made Eve, He made her to listen and follow Adam as he led. The reality is that if you are not talking enough, or leading by example, it is going to be difficult for her to follow your lead in the relationship.

How to communicate with a woman. Communication is not yelling, cursing or fussing. Communication is listening, understanding, agreeing to disagree at times, and moving forward past issues before they turn into problems. Right now if you are having communication problems, STOP right now what you are doing and take her somewhere outside of the house to sit and talk. Tomorrow is not promised and you must do something different today to have different results in your relationship.

A gentle answer turns away wrath, but a harsh word stirs up anger. ~ Proverbs 15:1

The way of a fool seems right to him, but a wise man listens to advice. ~ Proverbs 12:16

Last, remember if no one is talking, no one is listening. Be the leader and lead by example to make sure that there is not a night that goes by with you two upset at each other. Never fight fire with fire. You fight it with water. Use love as your water, and when you do not know what else to say, just say "I love you."

3. A Man's Trust

What money is to a bank, trust is to a relationship. Trust requires an investment from the beginning. The first day you meet each other, you share details of your life, past, present and future. From that first day, your partner should trust you 100%. This is true for many cases. However, there are cases where people have insecurities from their past relationships that will lessen the amount of trust invested in the current relationship.

How to invest in your relationship to build trust. Today starts a new day, and we will first start there because if you cannot let go of the past, you will hinder your future each day that you remain in your current relationship. Being a man, I understand that men do not fall in love very easily and may only love less than a hand full of women within their lifetime. Nevertheless, you do not want to let the last woman mess it up for the next woman.

Trust in the Lord with all your heart and lean not on your own understanding. ~ Proverbs 3:5

DO – *It's time for you to start trusting God 100%, and not yourself. You have to learn that to reach your blessing, you have to learn a few lessons. Often we say that we trust God, but do we really? You need to pray every night, "God help me with trusting my woman. I trust you and I trust that you will provide what I need and remove the things that I do not." There is power in your words. Do this prayer for no less than 60 days. Sometimes we have to talk directly with God and let ourselves hear that we need to trust the woman in our lives no matter what the last woman has done. The trick to making yourself feel better is that you have to* *make yourself think differently. Encouragement in gospel music can help as well. Listen to it for the next 60 days, 100% of your days. Your spirit needs to be fed with something different, so your mind and emotions can have different results.*

DON'T – *Go through your woman's things for the next 60 days. You have to start trusting God and not just her. What happens in the dark always comes to light and God has a way of exposing us to things. Do not question her about her whereabouts or where she is going. This is important because if you already have trust issues, you are probably already asking her 21 questions every time that she leaves the house. The less you ask, the more she will tell because you are doing something different.*

"I will say of the Lord, "He is my refuge and my fortress, my God in whom I trust." ~ Psalm 91:2

When trust is lost, how to rebuild it. The Lord will protect your heart and feelings, once you start trusting Him. Now it is time to start investing in the relationship, if you have lost trust by doing something on your end. You can work days and hours, trying to gain trust and lose it within seconds by doing something stupid. The interesting thing about women is if you have done something in error and she is still around, it means that she is holding onto the good in you. This lives within her feelings and not her mind. Her mind is probably telling her to leave, but her heart is keeping her there. Regaining trust starts in the mind, because you already have her heart.

DO – *Cut off all your friends and family right now. You might think this is crazy, but if this woman is your wife, future wife or you view her as your world, it is time for you to start acting like it. Cutting people off does not mean you do not need to talk to them, but it means you need to give her ALL OF YOUR ATTENTION. Remember the mind is everything, and you need to feed her mind with the* *two most important vessels on her body, her eyes*

and ears. Her eyes need to see you all the time.

That is why it is important to cut people off. The

more you leave her alone, the more her mind sits

idle and has time to think about the things you

have or have not done. You might think that you

will have to do this for the rest of your life, but in

reality, you will only have to do it for maybe

30days-60 days. After this, you cannot go back to

your old ways because they will bring back old

habits. She needs to see love, and she needs to see

that you really care and really want her to forgive

you.

How to get over the hump of infidelity.

Roses and cards are nice, but you need to do more

thoughtful things. For example, wash the clothes,

cook here and there, or clean up the house.

Writing her a love letter once a week will help a lot

also. Women love to read things about love and

what better way to read about love than to read

how you love her. Next, you need to have her at church as much as possible, so God can restore her heart as well. God has your back and if you ask for forgiveness, He will give you what you ask. Her ears need to now hear different things as much as possible. Yes, she will keep bringing up what you did time and time again, but it is important that you do not get frustrated and you fight her words with Love. When she throws it in your face, you need to just be quiet, or just say, "I love you, and I always will and we will get through this."

DO - Next, you need to leave and go turn on some gospel music to change the atmosphere in the house. She would have to have some strong, mean demon in her to come cursing and fussing at you while Gospel music is on. Remember, we must change the things she is hearing to change her thoughts, which will change her feelings. If you maintain this for at least two weeks, her throwing it up in your face will decrease. Give her access to everything you own. Cell phones, Facebook, Twitter, email or whatever else you have codes on. You made the mistakes, so now you have to invest back into her to gain that trust back. She will probably go through your things, but that will last for only maybe a week or two once she sees that you are not doing anything and spending all of your time with her. Make sure that during this process, you are using the methods in the communication chapter. That is, go somewhere to talk for an hour, have date nights and spend as much time outside of the house together as possible. This is the key to gaining the trust back. Keep her mind busy and in time, her insecurities shall pass too.

"Commit your way to the Lord; trust in Him and He will do this: He will make your righteousness shine like the dawn, the justice of your cause like the noonday sun." ~ Psalm 37:5-6

What is the root to trust. In relationships,
it is important to keep God at the core and not
have it just be about you and her. Including other
people always adds confusion and sometimes
create insecurities in your mind and in hers. Your
woman being your best friend makes her all of
what you need, all of your desires, and all that you
will have. The more time you spend with her is
your investment in your relationship. The less time
you spend with her is like you withdrawing money
out of the bank, so your balance lessens. The most
important element to trust is time. If you do not
remember anything else, and it seems the trust is
fading away and she starts to question your every
move, it's really simple. Just start spending more
time with her.

4. A Man's Love

One of the key ingredients to a relationship is Love. Many ask, "What is love?" We all have many different answers, and many different thoughts, but the important thing is how you display love.

What is love? Anyone can say, "I love you" but the question is do they really mean it, and are they really showing it? There are many important things to know about love and the main one is God. *"Love is patient, love is kind, it does not envy, it does not boast, it is not proud. It is not rude, it is not self-seeking, it is not easily angered, it keeps no record of wrongs. Love does not delight in evil but rejoices with the truth. It always protects, always trusts, always hopes always perseveres. Love never fails." ~ 1 Corinthians 13:4-8*

As a man, it is important that you practice God's word on Love. At times you will not understand your woman, but there will be more times that you will. Keep God and love at the core of the relationship.

DO – Be more patient in understanding her. Most women only want what is right for you and the relationship. To love her more, you must listen first, understand second, and speak last.

When love is lost, how to regain it. You might be in a situation where you feel like you have fallen out of love with your lady. You do not look at her the same or even know how to get that old love back that you two had in the beginning. There is always a root to the problem and I have the answer.

DO - Love is an action, not just a word. The way you fall in love again, is by doing things to reignite that fire. First, you need to write a one page letter about what were the things that made you ask her to become your woman, next in that letter include significant, relevant items: Where you first met, first kiss, first time you told her you loved her and how would you feel if she was out of your life. To feel something you have lost, you will need to jog your memory. Remember your mind controls everything, and what you think, will be what you feel. The only way you can feel something that is lost, is to go back to find it. After you write the letter, you need to buy something sentimental for her. The reason for this is to see her face light up. Your mind will tell your feelings, "This is why I fell in love with her." Not because of the money that was spent, but the smile on her face and the way you always made her feel.

How to take love to the next level.

To feel love, you must give love fully. You cannot try to be positive, but keep saying negative things. The mind and body just does not work like that. Once again, you need to get back to the foundation of the relationship and that is communication. Talking more will help you with understanding, and give you back those feelings.

"Above all, love each other deeply, because love covers over a multitude of sins. ~ 1 Peter 4:8"

Issues will always come up in relationships when you have two people with two different thoughts and minds. The key is how you handle these issues and this also determines if they turn into problems. If you know for a fact that your woman has fallen out of love with you, and is not showing you that she loves you anymore or your love life is just lost, today starts the day to fix it.

DO – *Get off your butt and ask her, "If this was a perfect world, what would make you happy?" Her answer will give you about a 75% chance of fixing the problem right away. One of the main things to fixing a situation is to just listen and apply. Unless your woman wants you to go buy a $1000 hand bag and you are just not that type of $1000 bag-buying type of guy, anything can be fixed with just listening. Always tell her you will try to do whatever it is she would like you to do to make her happy. NEVER promise! Promises are made to be broken, and if you slip one bit, you will be putting yourself in a worse situation than what you were in before. Women like to be active doing things, being shown off in public and acknowledged. Get her out of the house as much as possible, even if it is just going to church, the park or a Starbucks. Remember 90% of fights take place in the home, so the more you get her out of the house, the better.*

"There is no fear in love. But perfect love drives out fear, because fear has to do with punishment. The one who fears is not made perfect in love. ~ 1 John 4:18"

Stop holding on to the past, love keeps no record of wrong doing. If you are still here with her today, it starts a new day and you need to give 150% today. It is you and her against the world! If you are not ready to give her your all right now, you might as well end the relationship. Fear can hold your relationship back from growing into something beautiful. Let go and let God.

DON'T- *Keep bringing up issues or problems. You cannot change them, and there is no reason to give them energy at this point. Fight fire with water and use love as your water. Do not compare her to your past lovers. God made everyone different for a reason and she is probably the best thing that has happened to you if you open your eyes. If you are not working on the relationship, the relationship* *will continue to work against you. Stop leaving dead air in your relationship. If you have not fixed the last issue, fix it now because when the next issue comes up, you will be faced with having to deal with two issues at one time. Stop being hard and stand up. This is your WOMAN we are talking about. Show her things you have not shown her yet. You have nothing to lose but everything to gain at this point.*

"For where your treasure is, there your heart will be also. ~ Matthew 6:21"

How to rekindle the fire. If all else fails, turn your love life over to God. God is love, the creator of men and women, and with God there is no failure. Sometimes we want things so bad and force them on our partner, and they still do not work out. When this happens, it is time for you to let the love of Jesus place His hands in your relationship.

DO – Commit to your church and God as much as possible. Attend church, join a ministry, listen to gospel music 100% of your day and put it in God's hands. I am not telling you, "Oh now your life is bad, give your life to Jesus." But what I am telling you is that God is the source when it comes to love and the closer you come to Him, the closer He will come in your situation. Love is not prideful. Put down your pride, so He can fix your situation.

Love is the salt and pepper to your relationship. Without it, your relationship, like food, will be bland and nasty. No one wants to be in an unhappy relationship. Add some flavor to it by increasing the love. Do whatever it takes, in the name of love.

5. A Man's Compromise

One of the keys to longevity is Compromise. As a man, we want to have our way or dominate the relationship to just feel like the man, but the truth is a happy woman makes a happy home. This does not mean that she should have her way 24-7 around the clock, but this does mean that most women just want the best for you.

How to deal with giving and taking. You might also find yourself in a situation where you cannot get your woman to compromise on anything. She feels like it is her way or the highway. There is some ways this situation can change for the best on your behalf, however. **"A patient man has great understanding, but a quick-tempered man displays foolishness. ~ Proverbs 14:29**

The do's and don'ts to compromising.

DO- Take her somewhere, just you and her with no distractions. You must remember it is not about what you say, but how you say it. The key word you want to use is "Build." Tell her, "I love you, and I would like our relationship to go to the next level. I know I will not have all the right answers, but with us working TOGETHER and BUILDING on our future we can make this work. I want you to trust me as your man to make some decisions, just like I trust you as my woman to make decisions. I feel like our relationship is one sided, your way or the highway, but I just want to be happy too. I am here to make sure you are happy and our happiness should be a two way street. For us to take this to the next level, I need you to compromise a little more, just like I will compromise for you. I love you and can we work on BUILDING this?"

Women are very emotional, sensitive people. When you take the time to have a private discussion that identifies your commitment to improve the relationship, she will listen, understand and be willing to apply. The main ingredient in compromise is communication. You have to make sure you talk to her so that she can understand the importance on what you want within the relationship and how you feel things should change. You may currently feel like you two are always bumping heads. It is time to ask yourself, "Am I compromising?" There are several ways you can find out if you are truly compromising.

DO – *Ask her, "Do you feel like I always have to have my way? Do you feel like I compromise? What are some things you think I could do to make our relationship better? If this was a perfect world what would make you happy?"*

Asking questions concerning the relationship is always the easiest way to fix issues with compromise. The one thing about asking specific questions is that you will always get an answer from a woman that 99.9% of the time will be the truth. When dealing with a woman also, there are things to avoid when trying to get her to compromise.

"So in everything, do to others what you would have them do to you. ~ Matthew 7:12"

DON'T - *Make demands! No matter how much of a man you are, no grown person likes to be bossed around. It is better to lead by example.*

Why is compromising important. Show her how her compromising can help the relationship grow. Avoid trying to get her to compromise on things you already know she has not been doing since day 1. For example, if there are certain things sexually she never did in the beginning, do not expect for her to all of sudden compromise and do these things daily. Another example is that if she was not washing her car or the dishes and you always did it, do not expect for that to just change overnight. Now these things can change if you would like them to, but it takes time and patience. The key is that you must compromise on something that you were also not doing in the beginning, so that you can lead by example.

How to compromise and not lose your respect. If you do not remember anything, always remember relationships are give and take. Sometimes you have to give, just so you can take. If you feel like you are always giving, and she is taking, it is time to have that 1 hour talk to change some things. Your happiness is just as important as hers. There is no room for selfishness in relationships. Either work on it, or you will be working each other out of the door.

6. A Man's Pride and Ego

Every man's pride and ego can be the gift and the curse. It can save you or hinder you, and when it comes to relationships, it has to go. Your woman will know you inner, dark secrets that no one else will know. She will know your flaws, imperfections and your short comings. For your relationship to grow, let the pride and ego go.

When to let go of your pride and ego. What you have to realize is that you are not less of a man to your woman when you show your soft side, when you show her that you care more about her at times than yourself, and that her happiness is just as important as yours. Trust that I understand coming into the relationship you probably had or may still have a huge ego. If you are struggling with it, here are some methods to help you.

"Do nothing out of selfish ambition or vain conceit, but in humility consider others better than yourselves. Each of you should look not only to your own interests, but also to the interests of others. Your attitude should be the same as that of Christ Jesus." ~ Philippians 2:3-5

DO – *Come to your woman humbly and ask, "Are there things that you think I am too prideful about that you feel affects our relationship? Do you think my ego gets in the way of decisions I make for our relationship?"*

The best way to change anything in your relationship is to go to the source that sees and talks to you daily. Trust and believe your woman will give you an honest answer because she had been waiting on this moment for a long time. If you do this, it will help your relationship grow.

Remember, she will mirror you and if she sees you are trying to change, she will start to change also.

DON'T- *Get upset when she tells you the truth. These are things that will help the both of you. Most of the time, you will not see the problems because you cannot see yourself every day, but she does.*

"If a house is divided against itself, that house cannot stand." ~ Mark 3:25

"Better a patient man than a warrior, a man who controls his temper than one who takes a city." ~ Proverbs 16:32

What pride and ego does to the relationship. Issues will always come up, but how you handle them determines if they turn into problems. Most of the time, they can turn into problems because of your ego and pride. Your pride and ego at times will not allow you to let go of the same issue, so you both can move forward, but you must realize it is hindering your relationship day by day. I understand sometimes you feel that you are not wrong and your ego tells you to just sit there and stay angry at her, but what is that fixing? The problem will still be there when you are done being upset.

"Refrain from anger and turn from wrath; do not fret – it leads only to evil." ~ Psalm 37:8

DO - *Try, even when you know you're not wrong to tell her, "I love you, let's move forward and make sure this doesn't happen again." This will help with your pride and let her know, you are not full of yourself and not willing to let your pride down.*

When is having pride and ego important.

Pick your battles. When your pride is hurt, let her know. People cannot read minds and it is better than just walking around angry. The more she knows the better. Your woman will always respect you as her man as long as you do, and that is talking to her instead of listening to your ego. Women were created to love, care and become our help mates. Do not be afraid to show her your loving side. Women love that. If you are currently seeking to date a woman, your ego is very important when you first meet her. It dictates the tone of where the relationship could go.

"As it is, you boast in your arrogance. All such boasting is evil." ~ James 4:16

DON'T- *Be boastful. For some women, it is a turn off. For others, they will use you for whatever you are boasting about. Do not always talk about yourself. Let her talk as well. This way, you can learn more of her and she can learn of you. While listening to each other, make sure you tell her what you are looking for. If you are looking for a relationship, it is important that she knows this. If she does not, it can destroy your pride as you are trying to develop something with her.*

"Thru says the Lord: 'Let not the wise man boast
in his wisdom, let not the mighty man boast in his
might, let not the rich man boast in his riches.'" ~
Jeremiah 9:23

The cause and effect from pride and ego.
Everyone is prideful at some point or another, but
today starts a new day and do not let that be an
excuse on why your relationship cannot progress.
You hold the keys to your relationship as a man.
You can position where the relationship goes, if
you just let go of your pride and ego. Sometimes
you just have to truly take a look in the mirror, and
ask yourself, "Do I really want my relationship?" If
the answer is yes, start making changes.

7. A Man's Value and Worth

When God created Adam, He placed his stamp on the earth that men would be great, if they stayed faithful to Him and obeyed His commands.

What's your worth in the relationship. It is important as a man that you know what you bring to the table. In the same sense, you cannot abuse this. Women look up to men for security, strength, guidance and to just be a man.

When she doesn't value you, how to gain it back. You could be at a point in your life where you are not feeling valued, and you are feeling like your woman just does not know your worth. Here are some things to do to gain these things back.

DO - *Ask questions. It is going to take YOU to throw your pride out of the window to get to the root of why she does not value you. Her disvaluing is on the same lines of her not respecting you, so this is an important fix. Her words might cut like a knife, but you need the truth. With this in mind, ask, "If this were a perfect world, what could I do to help you appreciate me?" As a woman, she may list and provide details on many issues. You need to make the choice to either try to do them or leave.*

 Knowing what you bring to the table as a man. Sometimes this disvalue could come from things you did in the past, even though you have now left those bad behaviors behind. Or, it can come from her simply running over you from the beginning, so this was something you may have created. It can be turned around, but it is going to take actions, effort and her realizing what you bring to the table.

How to show her you value her. In long term relationships, people get very comfortable and get used to routines. Your woman might be at a point where she does not feel valued and continues to complain over and over again. You might feel that, "I'm happy the way we are and have been." But what you do not realize is that she is not. Women see their friends and coworkers doing things that they dream of and things that they wish you, as their mate would do just once for them. Guess what? It is time for you to show her that you value her.

DO - *for the next 90 days, 1 time a week you need to do something that shows your love for her publicly. For example- Send roses to her job, put roses on her car, take her out to eat and have the waitress bring over her favorite color dress or shoes. It just needs to be in the public. I understand you feel like, "Why do I need to do all these extra things in public?" What you must* *realize is at this point that it is not about you. It is about her.*

Women like attention and sometimes like to share with their friends the special actions you may do on their behalf. Showing them special attention in different circumstances is the gift that will keep giving. A happy woman makes a happy life. This will increase the action in the bedroom, smiles on her face and those little days you want to yourself to watch the game. She will leave you alone and later make you your favorite meal.

Even when dating, it is important to notice when a woman has value for you in the beginning. She cooks for you, washes your clothes and goes all out for you and you two are doing nothing but just dating. This could go one or two ways, so be careful. 1. If you make her your woman, great. Your relationship can grow into something even better. 2. If you are just playing around, you are going to destroy her in the end. One day you must remember the shoe will be on the other foot, so be careful in the beginning when you are meeting women. If she is doing a lot and you know you do not want a relationship with her, tell her to slow down. Do not keep letting her proceed to cater to you. While being single, just focus on being a good man so that God can send you a great woman.

8. A Woman's Relationship with God

As a woman, God purposed you to be a wife. You are to be a helpmate and to reproduce.

Why your relationship with God is important. Your relationship with God is as important as the relationship your man has with God also. Even though the roles are different, the impact is the same. Through the midst of storms in your relationship, it is your responsibility to uplift your man and when he falls short, to supply him with strength.

"I will make him a helper suitable for him" ~ Genesis 2:18

"A wife of noble character who can find? She is worth far more than rubies. Her husband has full confidence in her and lacks nothing of value. She

brings him good, not harm, all the days of her life. She selects wool and flax and works with eager hands. She is like the merchant ships, bringing her food from afar. She gets up while it is still dark; she provides food for her family and portions for her servant girls. She is clothes with strength and dignity; she can laugh at the days to come. She speaks with wisdom, and faithful instruction is on her tongue. She watches over the affairs of her household and does not eat the bread of idleness. Her children arise and call her blessed; her husband also, and he praises her. Many women do noble things, but you surpass them all. Charm is deceptive, and beauty is fleeting; but a woman who fears the Lord is to be praised. Give her the reward she has earned, and let her works bring her praise at the city gate." – Proverbs 31:10-31

How to get your man on the same page when it comes to God. God knew Adam needed

Eve to complete his purpose after He supplied him with a job. As James Brown said, "It's a man's world, but it's nothing without a woman." You play an important part to the success or the failure of the relationship. Submission is a must, but do not just submit to any man. Most women err when they become submissive to the wrong men and are left wondering why the relationship did not progress. You might ask, "How do I avoid this?"

DON'T – *Hang out in the clubs and say that you want a Godly man. Pay attention to the men you date. If he has a worldly mind, he is going to give you worldly actions. If he was not going to church when you met him, the only person that will get him there is God at this point. Stop believing everything you hear a man say, and start believing what he shows you. Stop being so quick to have sex with men. The faster you give it up, the faster your value goes down. Sex does not equal love. God* *equals love. Stop idolizing the men that you are dating. We serve a jealous God and the only man you should honor is your husband.*

DO – *Attend church if you are single. This includes bible study and joining a ministry. Just like Eve was easily deceived, you will be also. You need to have your heart as close to God as possible so that He can provide you with the man that will take care of it. If you are married and your family falls off from going to church, get them back there; even if you have to start going by yourself or just with the kids. God will get your husband back there, but you have to maintain your relationship with Him so that God can go to work on your husband. Get on your knees and pray every night even if your husband is lying in the bed looking at you crazy. Your prayers are direct communication with God and He will deliver. You just need to be still.*

What's your purpose. God created you to follow your husband's lead. You need to make sure he is a leader. Make sure he is submissive to God, before you take the relationship any step further. Everything has to be aligned correctly for the foundation of the house to become a home. Just because you go to church and bible study every week, does not make a house a home. You are missing the key element of the home and that is the husband. If you are currently in a relationship and your man does not want to go to church and does not have a relationship with God, it is time for you to sit down and take a look at your relationship and decide. "Should I continue with this relationship? Will he change? Is it worth it?" Ask yourself these things because as a woman of God, you have a relationship with God. Will your husband have the same? Will he be able to lead? Most marriages end in divorce because when the woman says "Yes" to the ring, she forgets all of the things needed for the marriage to work. Marriage is the goal. When you make that commitment to become his woman, you want a marriage filled with happiness, joy and peace. Not a marriage filled of misery, doubt and unhappiness.

DON'T - *Hold onto a man for comfort. If the relationship is not right, it is going to carry over to the marriage. Marriage does not fix problems. It just prolongs them and makes the situation complicated. Remember if he does not know God and love God, it is going to be hard for him to understand the true meaning of marriage.*

When the relationship is going through a storm, how to get God involved. Your relationship with God can and will always get you back to the basics. As Christians, we are often living in the world and not of the world, so it is very easy to fall off track. You were taught the spiritual basics and may have practiced them regularly before your husband came along. Be sure you refer back to them when you have nothing else to turn to.

DON'T – *Turn to friends and family. This does not always give you the resolution that you need and often introduces bias that does not get to the root of the problem. They may not always be willing and able to offer sound advice without being overcritical of your partner or you. They are not God. There is nothing wrong with seeking help from a professional counselor. Someone on the outside that does not know either of you can help fix the simple problems. Social media does not need to know about your problems also. It cannot fix problems either. Marriage will not be perfect, but the less other people know about your issues, the better.*

At times you might want to give up and feel like it is impossible to fix the marriage or relationship, but with God all things are possible. Put God first and He will provide you with everything you need in your life.

9. A Woman's Communication

A gentle answer turns away wrath, but a harsh word stirs up anger. ~ Proverbs 15:1

It is not what you say, but how you say it. This is the key to communication as a woman. You know how to naturally talk, but listening is more important.

How to learn when it's best to listen and not talk. Most of you may have a man that does not like to talk or express himself. There is a root to this problem, and it could be the way that you communicate with him.

DO – *When he starts to talk, just listen, and take 10-15 seconds to think, gain understanding and then speak. This is important because men are very simple and simple minded. We do not complicate what we are saying and there is no secret way of decoding it. Just listen to what he says word for* *word because there is some truth in his words. It does not matter if what he says hurts your feelings or puts a smile on your face. Avoid answering a question with a question. You may be trying to get him to just reword what he already told you, which can cause anger. He may then not want to talk about certain subject matters. Agree to disagree when issues come up that are not resolved quickly, and say something positive before negative. The way a man's mind work is when he hears the negatives, it is heard as a nag, but when he hears the positive first, he will understand that you just have something to talk to him about.*

Everyone should be quick to listen, slow to speak and slow to become angry. ~ James 1:19

Anger comes from the lack of understanding within the communication. Within the first 6 months of the relationship, believe what you see from your man so that you will have no reason to think otherwise. Understanding is gained by his actions leading up to his words. Remember you cannot change a man, only God can do that. Using good communication methods can help you ease the issues and avoid problems.

DON'T- *Avoid using curse words when talking to a man. It displays anger, ignorance and this can cause more problems when using foul language that can heighten the tension during a discussion rather than diffuse it. The power of life and death is in the tongue. If you speak with curse words, then he is going to respond with curse words. The conversation will never go anywhere. You might say "It is not me. It is him that uses the curse words." Do not fight fire with fire. You fight fire with water. The water is within your words. Respond to hate with love, and not more hate. Tell him "I love you, I love you" over and over again in the midst of his talking. God is love and love conquers all. He will either shut up or calm down in* *time. Remember, you have to do different things to have different results.*

The importance of communication. At the beginning of the relationship is the best time to establish talking and listening to each other whole heartedly because you can learn more from each other over time. The will positively impact the time you are having a future discussion on issues that may occur, because they will. No matter how perfect you feel that you are for each other, the reality about life is that you are two humans with two different minds and will think alike on some things and think different on most things. The key is meeting in the middle and compromising.

DO - Spend 1-2 days a week to just talk for 1 hour. No distractions, no phones, no Facebook, no Twitter, and no children. Just the two of you. With technology being the ruler of communication today, we as people do not talk directly to each other anymore. We use email, Facebook, text and talking

*on the phone to talk without more face to face. DO
NOT do this exercise in the house. Most fights,
arguments take place within the home or even in
the car, so avoid doing methods in the car as well.
Go to a park, Starbucks, just somewhere outside of
your home. The way you think is the way you feel
and control your reactions. In the household when
the littlest thing may be said in a negative way to
get a point across, the mind triggers that an
argument is about to start so the body gets on the
defense and your actions will cause you to be ready
to respond inappropriately and not listen first and
then try to understand second. Also, it will be kind
of hard to fight outside on a nice sunny beautiful
day, so do this exercise outside your home as much
as possible.*

  How to communicate with a man. Now
you might be asking, "What do we talk about?"
Good question. The very first day you need to go
back down memory lane. Talk about the first date,

the first time you two met, the first time for everything, and the first time you told him you loved him. It is important to begin the first day off like this because it will set the tone of this exercise. The next day talk about anything that comes to mind, but stay away from anything negative like the past. Focus on the future, current events, building with each other, new advantages, new plans, outside the box thoughts, and things you never told each other.

DO - *You should do the 1-hour one on one exercise for a minimum of 90 days, but it would not hurt to do this for the rest of your lives because you will always learn something new about each other.*

He who answers before listening, that is his foolishness and his shame. ~ Proverbs 18:13

How to get through to him, when he won't say a word. If no one is talking, no one is listening. You might feel at times that you are the best communicator and he is just not listening at all to what you have to say. This is very common, but there are ways of fixing this.

DON'T - *Complain that he is not listening; just do things to get his attention.*

DO - *Write him letters about how you feel, but always keep them positive. Remember men can have a one track mind, so the letter leaves him no choice but to read it. You might be thinking, "What if he just throws it away? Or just doesn't read it?" It is simple; do not respond with evil or hate. Respond with love instead. Write another letter with nothing but 3 big words, "I LOVE YOU". If you plan on staying in the relationship, you need to give 150% all of the time. It is VERY important that you two use the 1 hour talking method. It will help avoid your relationship getting to this point. If you still cannot get through to him, play the gospel music loud in the house to set a different atmosphere in your home in order to open up the communication lane. Once you see a difference in*

him, then it is time for you to start talking again,
but NOT about anything negative. Everything said
should be positive about what he has done lately
and some things that you would like to do
differently to help the both of you.

You will have your issues in the relationship,
but how you handle the issues determines if they
turn into problems. Communication is everything;
it causes problems or decreases them. When all
else fails, always talk to him no matter what is
going on because when you leave space, you leave
opportunity.

10. A Woman's Trust

Trust is one of the hardest things to gain back once it is lost. As a woman you have probably dealt with your share of heart breaks, cheaters, liars and deceivers. Today starts a new day because God has you reading this book and wants you to move forward.

When trust is lost, how to rebuild it. First, if you are still in the relationship with the guy that has caused you to have trust issues, it is time to make a choice. Either you need to give 150% and try to forgive so you can move forward, or walk away from the relationship, so you can be restored and have happiness. Trust issues start and end mentally. If you keep doing the same things in your relationship, even when he is trying to help you forgive him, you will never move forward. If you have a choice to stay it is time to start trusting God and not yourself.

Trust in the Lord with all your heart and lean not on your own understanding. ~ Proverbs 3:5

How to get over the hump of infidelity. You cannot go back and change what he has done or said, so there is no need to talk about it. When you keep talking about the past, you are giving it more energy than it deserves and replanting the past back into your head over and over again. Next, you need to start talking about the future and nothing of the past.

DO – *You both need to attend church together so God can go to work on your heart. Tell your man you love him daily. You need to do this so your ears can hear you love him, your mind will think about it and your feelings will start to change from bad to good. The trick is changing your mind and you will* *be able to change your feelings. Tell him out of your mouth, "I forgive you." Pray every night out loud, "God help me move forward, restore my heart, I am trusting in you now and not myself, guide my steps." There is power in your words and there is power in your prayers, use this method for the next 60 days.*

DON'T - *Go through his phone, email, Facebook, Twitter or anything that you use to try to go through. It is no point at this point, if you are trying to move forward. You must trust God and not yourself. If he is still cheating or doing anything wrong, God will expose it to you. Meanwhile, you just need to commit to Him and work on moving forward. You must change the things you are looking at and hearing to change your feelings with trust and it starts with your eyes not going through his things.*

> ***How to let go and move forward.*** You always have a choice if you cannot trust your man

anymore, and that is to leave. We all know this, but always look for the good in every person. It is time that you lean on God and the good in him so you can move forward. If you were the one that has now lost the trust by cheating, flirting or just having a hard time getting your man to trust you, it is time for you to do different things.

DO- *One thing about trust is realizing has your man really trusted you from day one. If you have not given him your full attention, it is time. It is time to stop running your mouth on the phone with all your friends, hanging out with them and running the streets with your home girls. The way you gain trust or gain back trust is investing time. This does not mean having sex with him 24-7, but sitting and watching his favorite sports team play even if you do not understand what is going on. Going to the gym with him, even if you do not feel the need to work out and just being available for the relationship. Give him access to all your things.*

Including, cell phone, email, Facebook, Twitter and whatever you have passwords on. Trust, he will not go through them no longer than 1 week or two. Once you give people access to things, they are less likely to go through your things anyway, but it gives them a sense of security. Changing your number will not hurt things anyway. Fresh starts always refresh the relationship to move forward in the right direction.

DON'T – *Nag, fight, become angry, negative or anything that does not give off positive vibes. Remember you always have a choice and that is to leave, but if you choose to stay, know that it is time to let down the pride and try some different things. That includes investing in your man.*

"It is better to take refuge in the Lord than to trust in man. ~ Psalm 118:8

Holding on to your past is doing nothing but hindering your future. Just because the last guy hurt you, cheating and lied to you does not mean your current man is. If you choose to move forward it is time to let go and let God. People are placed in our lives by design, and not just because. Some people will be lessons, leading us to our blessings. The day you choose to let go of your past, will be the day you will control your future. You cannot go back and change anything, so today let's start a new beginning heading toward your future.

DO- *Throw away everything that you had of your past relationships. That includes pictures, phone numbers, delete and block on Facebook & Twitter, throwing away clothes that remind you of him, selling that engagement/wedding ring that you have been holding onto. It is time that everything of his to go. You cannot move forward, if you do not mentally start letting go of the things you are holding onto. Remember, he has already moved on with his life and it is time you start to move on.*

Any time you start having trust issues, talk to your man and not your friends or family. Friends and family is the first people that make the situation worse than what it is. Even if you do not feel like you can talk to him, you need to still try because it is not what you say, but how you say it.

DO – *Tell him what is making you not trust him. Paint pictures so he can see the cause and effects. For example: He goes out and stays out all night long, and you have an attitude for the whole next day and do not cook, have sex or anything the next day because of him staying out late, which causes trust issues and the effect you gaining an attitude.*

What is the root of trust. Last, some situations get out of control with being disrespectful. You will have to make good judgment calls. Trust issues are like burns from a fire. You have 1st degree, which the skin goes back to normal. 2nd degree where the mark will still be there and 3rd where you were burned to a degree where you might need surgery or it will take a long time for you to heal and recover. If your trust issues are at a 3rd degree, it might be best to walk away. You need time to heal and start back over. You have to remember that as long as you have God, you are never alone. He is a restorer and if you are at that 3rd degree burn with trust in your relationship, commit to Him as much as possible in these next 90 days and God will give you the answer on what you need to do.

11. A Woman's Love

Food, water and air are the things we need to live. And Love is the main thing that we need for a relationship to live. Love gives a relationship hope when issues and problems start to happen.

What is love? Love is the greatest feeling in the world when everything is going right, and can be the worst feeling in the world when things are going wrong. Love can be an addiction like a drug and it can have you on a high like the strongest drug in the world. Today it is time to fix the love that might have been lost or increase the love to another level.

"Love is patient, love is kind. It does not envy, it does not boast, it is not proud. It is not rude, it is not self-seeking, it is not easily angered, it keeps

no record of wrongs. Love does not delight in evil but rejoices with the truth. It always protects, always trusts, always hopes, always perseveres. Love never fails." ~ 1 Corinthians 13:4-8

When love is lost, how to regain it. Many times when love is lost, we never understand where we lost it so that we can find it again. Love does not just happen on its own. Whether you are trying to love your man or trying to fall back in love with him, it is going to take work. Right now you need to decide is the love worth it? Is love worth the fight? Will love provide happiness, peace and joy? If the answers are yes, then it is time to go to work! Even if you feel like he should be putting in the work to gain the love back in the relationship, you will also have a responsibility to uphold your part in the relationship and its renovation. It is always easy to just leave, but consider trying these things before you go.

"There is no fear in love. But perfect love drives out fear, because fear has to do with punishment. The one who fears is not made perfect in love." ~ 1 John 4:18

DO - *Show love, stop just saying it. No more complaining and nagging. If that is all you have been doing and it has not gotten you anywhere, you might as well try something different. If he hangs out with the boys too much, coming home late, not spending time with you and you want him to change those ways, start telling him when he leaves out the door, "Have a great time baby, be safe and I love you." Sounds crazy, huh? But what you must realize, when you start doing different things you will get different results. In his head, he will notice that you did not nag or complain, and start to think, "That was different, what's wrong with her?" You cannot keep fighting fire with fire, you have to fight it with water and that is love. Do* *this over and over, and in time he will start thinking you just do not care anymore.*

He will also start thinking now you either about to leave or seeing someone else. He will then start staying home more or even taking you out just because those insecurities will start creeping up in his own head. Now, in the midst of all this you must still increase the love just to add the cherry on the cake. Once a week, do something sentimental which includes a card, bear, writing a letter, taking him out to eat on your treat, making a candle light dinner, buying him a gift or anything that comes to mind to show your love.

How to take love to the next level. I know you are thinking that this is just crazy especially if you are dealing with a man that makes it hard for you to love him. But what do you have to lose? When you are in a relationship, you do nothing but mirror your partner. If he is making you upset with his actions, it makes it hard for you to show love toward him and in return it makes him continue to do whatever he has been doing, and he will continue to not care because neither of you are happy. Treat this method like a last minute sale and you will only have 10 minutes to get those favorite shoes you like. If you do not add some urgency to your relationship you are going to lose it. Do these things for at least 60 days to see if the relationship turns around. Also use the methods in the communication chapter as well.

How to rekindle the fire. For some couples that have been together for so many years and sometimes you question yourself if you are even in love any more. Do not worry; 9 out of 10 you probably still are, but you are just so comfortable in your ways that the flame has just gone out of the fire this is an easy fix and once again, it just takes a little effort on your end.

"Above all, love each other deeply, because love covers over a multitude of sins." ~ 1 Peter 4:8

"Greet one another with a kiss of love." ~ 1 Peter 5:14

DO - *Once a week you two need to plan a date night. Get out the house, have fun like you used to when you first met and started dating. Get out of your routine of just going to work, home and the kids. To maintain the flame of love in your relationship you have to make sure you keep pouring gasoline on that fire to keep it growing and growing. You should be wearing something sexy to bed at least once, if not twice a week. Start surprising him! Make the relationship back interesting again. Keep him guessing what could be next that she is going to do. Go buy a new wig and come to bed as someone else. You have to do different things to have different results.*

Most men feel love through you being affectionate and the little loving things women do. For example, the thoughtful cards, I love you notes and fixing his favorite meal by candle light. Turn on some romantic music riding in the car, laying in the house and cuddling in bed. Remember the mind is everything and two of the most important vessels are the eyes and ears. The eyes see different things, the ears hear different things, and the mind will think different things and the body will feel different ways. In the end, his actions will change and you two will start mirroring each other.

"Whoever does not love does not know God, because God is love." ~ 1 John 4:8

Even as being a single woman, it is important that you keep your mind open and heart filled with love so God can send you the man that will fulfill your needs. This is not the time to be bitter or jealous of other people relationships because your past relationship did not work out. Let your past be a lesson learned that will get you to your blessings. Let other people's successful relationships be the encouragement that can show you that true love is still alive and living. While being single, it is time to prepare yourself so when God sends him, you will be ready.

DO - *Stay away from bitter single women. They will just keep you down and bitter along with them. Stay away from negative people and negative places, they are not providing positive results. Stay sociable and approachable. It is important that you always keep a smile on your face so men will know it is OK to approach you. Commit to your church as much as possible. The closer you come to God, the closer He will come to you. Give yourself time to work on you and a better you will be for him. Last, remember stay patient, because love is.*

Above all, you need to make sure your relationship is always in the presence of the source of love, and that is God. Feelings are internal things that God can intervene and change at any given moment of your life. When everything seems to be going wrong, God can make it right just with your commitment. After reading this chapter, you need to look in the mirror and ask yourself, "Am I committed to God? Do I give him more of my time than just Sundays?" If the answers are no, get committed. God does not forsake the righteous and it is time for you to have everything God has purposed for you.

12. A Woman's Compromise

Longevity in any relationship is based on compromise. No relationship will last if it is always one-sided. It is OK if your man spoils you and give you your way on certain things, but what you must understand in time it is going to get old and he is going to need his way.

How to know if you're giving too much. The root to compromising is understanding. Take the time to understand his likes, dislikes and the things that keeps him happy.

"So in everything, do to others what you would have them do to you." ~ Matthew 7:12

DO - *1 day a week give your man his way; rather its watching sports or him going to play basketball. That day, join him. Even if you do not know what is* *going on while watching the sport, it will mean more to him than you know to have you there. It works the same way if you go watch him play basketball. Just think about how many times he has went to the mall with you, while you tried on 100 different outfits. Compromise works the same way.*

At times you might have been together for years and just got to a place of being comfortable. When these times happen, you might think you know what makes him happy, but there are some things that can take his happiness to another level. Remember, in a relationship you should mirror each other. His happiness can increase yours and your happiness can increase his.

DO – *Take him somewhere outside of the house and ask, "If this was a perfect world what would make you happy and what would keep you happy, be honest." He will probably smile and ask you, "Why are you asking this?", but you just reply, "I* *want our relationship to go to another level, so it's important I know these things."* This method will give you a mental note of the things you can do daily, weekly and monthly.

"Do anything without complaining or arguing." ~ Philippians 2:14

Why is compromising important. One of the toughest things as a woman is knowing when to SHUT UP! Every single issue does not need to be addressed. Learn how to pick your battles. The more nagging and complaining you do, the more you will push him away. It is not about what you say, but how you say it. Now, I am not saying just let him get away with murder, but if it is things he has been doing since day one and you guys have been together for years, chances are those things are just not going to change. Get use to them or try these methods to work on knocking that mountain down.

The do's and don'ts to compromising.

DON'T - *Make demands! No grown person likes be ordered around. Most men will get on the defensive once you put them in a corner and just do the same things they had been doing, but two times worse.*

DO - *Start off with something positive when you are addressing the issue. For example: "Baby, I love you. And I love having you in my life, but sometimes I feel like you go out too much. I just want to make sure we can grow together and not apart. I love you." When you start off with a positive, his mind will hear that first before all the things in between. It prepares him to receive what you have to say, and when you end it with a positive it reminds his mind of the first positive. Remember, what the mind thinks, the body feels and the results are the actions. To get better actions out of him you have to control what he sees and hears, because it is the only way his thought pattern will change. It is a process and it does not happen overnight, but if you* *practice this for at least 30-60 days, you will see change.*

How to compromise and not lose your respect. Just because he is the man does not mean everything has to be his way also. The hardest thing for a woman to do is letting her man be the man, but not giving him full control over her. This is an important part of compromise and this part roots back to the relationship with God. If he is led by the world and you see the relationship going down the wrong road, it makes it hard to compromise on things you know is not going to help you guys grow. Your relationship could already be at this point and you just truly do not know what to do and you feel like all you do is compromise all the time and are still not happy. Well, here is a solution.

DON'T- *Complain anymore. Sounds crazy, but if that is all that you have been doing, it is not going to help. All the things you been doing to make him* *happy and to keep him happy must decline. Happiness is a two way street in a relationship and he must understand your happiness is just important. Day by day, week by week you do this your relationship will go one or two ways. 1. He will notice the change and come ask you what's going on or why you change. At that point, you sit him down and say, "I love you a lot and I love seeing you happy, but I'm not feeling the same way that I'm proving to you. If you want me to go back to the old me making you happy, start thinking about making me happy sometimes." He either will be puzzled by this because he has forgot how to make you happy or it might be at a point where he just really does not care about your happiness. If he asks, "Well what will make you happy?" Just keep it simple, meaning; "Just watch a movie with me, wash the dishes every once and a while." You need to have a voice at this point, but do not ask for the world. You must crawl before you can walk. Now, the second way this can go. He could just be so caught up in whatever he is doing in life and truly do not even notice the change or even care. At this time, you need to make the biggest decision of your life and that is either to stay or leave.*

The reality about compromising is that sometimes your all might not be enough and your enough might not seem like your all. Only you know how much you can take and how much you can give. Try your best to compromise because that is the only way your relationship will last. If you feel like you gave your all, the last thing you need to do is not beat yourself up if you decide to leave. God knows, and you know you did your best.

13. A Woman's Pride and Ego

As a woman, a lot of your pride and ego is rooted to your past. The things that you have been through and experienced in the past play a part. If you are reading this right now, today starts a new day and you are not your past. Pride and ego can make or break a relationship when it comes to dealing with a man.

When to let go of your pride and ego. A man will die before letting his pride down sometimes, and if you hurt or disrespect his pride, it can be the end of the world. Two people together with too much ego can be a ticking time bomb ready to explode. You might feel like it is too late to change how you feel about your pride or even your man pride, but if you have life right now it is never too late.

"When pride comes, then comes disgrace, but with humility comes wisdom." ~ Proverbs 11:2

DO – *You and your man need to be on the same accord, and it is time for you to be the bigger person if you can. Take him somewhere to talk, outside of the house. All you need to say is, "I realize I have been kind of hard to deal with, but I would like to change. What are some things that you think I need to change?" This will be a direct question to him to help you with your pride. Yes, he will tell you the truth and it might hurt, but what do you have to lose at this point. You have everything to gain now when everything is out in the open and you leave your pride to listen. Remember, listening creates understanding and understanding creates growth.*

"Pride only breeds quarrels, but wisdom is found in those who take advice." ~ Proverbs 13:10

What pride and ego does to the relationship. In your relationship you might be running into a point where you are just hitting a brick wall with communication and understanding with your man. You need to ask yourself, do you think before you speak? Have you used words as weapons? If the answers are yes, then you have hurt his ego and pride totally and he has shut you out. This can be fixed; you just have to want to really want fix it!

DO – *Admit your wrongs and tell him you will do better. The key is actions, not just words because words are just words without actions. You must change things mentally to change how you use words and the way you talk to him. For the next 30 days you need to listen to gospel music 100% of your day. Music is a reflection of our thoughts and speech. If you listen to curse word filled music 24-7,* *chances are you will start speaking it. Start listening to gospel music and it will help you replace those words with positive words. Also, for the next 30 days, no more drama reality shows. What you see, you think, and then speak! Just because you see those women on TV talking and acting crazy does not mean it is OK for you to do it. Your man might let you get away with it, but it is only going to last for so long. Talk and spend more time with him rather than your friends. Sometimes the people we hang out with or talk to, influence our thoughts with their lives or the way they go about life whether it is negative or positive. To restore his pride, you need to cater to him and show that you are willing to fix this matter. You two also need to be in as many positive environments as possible. For example - Church, parks, social events for couples, and places that can keep you two laughing. Laughing and having fun is good for the soul; it helps you forget about all the wrong doing.*

DON'T- *Blame him for your actions. You always have a choice to stay or leave. Two wrongs don't make it right. If he has done things in the past and now he is acting right, but you have not let it go and that resentment is filled in your heart, you need to make a decision of trying everything to fix it or leave. If you are not willing to give 150% no matter what happened in the past, you are just hindering your future.*

"The end of a matter is better than its beginning, and patience is better than pride." ~ Ecclesiastes 7:8

Being a single woman with a lot of pride can keep you single for a long time. Not saying you need to lower your standards to have someone, but the last thing a man want is a woman whose pride has her hard up and bitter from her past. It is OK to have standards, but do not let it show in your pride. It is important while being a single woman to connect yourself with God as much as possible because when he sends that man your way, you do not need your pride running him off.

The cause and effect from pride and ego.

Your ego might tell you, "Not to deal with a man with 2-3 kids" but this man could have had twins, is a widow, and a great father ready to get married. You just will never know until you put your pride and ego out the way to find out. You will never know where your next blessing will come from by just listening, understanding and giving a man a chance. Remember, no one is perfect, not even you. When you meet someone new, put the ego aside and give them a chance to tell their story.

14. A Woman's Value and Worth

When Eve was created, she was created for Adam; not Adam for Eve. This would suggest that as a woman, you are worth so much to a man and the success that he may obtain.

Knowing your worth. To keep your worth, everything starts in the beginning when you meet.

DON'T - *Have sex on the first night meeting a man. The longer you hold out with sex, the better. Remember when you have sex the situation is either going to go left or right, and 9 times out of 10, it will go left before it goes right. Cooking, cleaning and doing things as a wife if it is just a man you are dating is a no go. These simple things that might be common sense to some women are disvaluing you every single time you do it. It is like*

you are playing cards and showing your opponent
your hand. He will need to earn these things over
time.

How to make sure your man values you.
You might feel like if you are not doing a lot, you
will lose him to another women that is doing all of
these things. The reality of the situation is the
more you do in the beginning, you give him nothing
to look forward to. Even if he is just your
"boyfriend", there is still a limit to the things you
should not and should do.

DON'T - *Move in with your boyfriend. It will make*
him very comfortable and content. The problem
that happens with this is it does not give him
anything to look forward to because you are giving
him everything without him making a commitment
to becoming your husband.

DO - *Show him you appreciate him as being a good*
man. You can show your appreciation by spending

time with him, occasionally taking him out on a date and paying the bill, watching sports with him and being very supportive to the things he needs help with. Being a good woman does not mean you have to play "Wifey" without being the wife. It means you show him what he could have with effort and actions.

What you should do when value is lost.
Every woman starts with a value chart of 10. Every time he lies and you take him back it devalues by 1. If he cheats, it goes down by 2. If he spends late nights out and do not give a care about you caring, it goes down by 3. Before you know it, you are down to being valued at 1 out of 10, and you are unhappy, bitter and hurt. If this person is you, here are some things to do.

DO - *Take 3 pieces of paper, and label them pros and cons. 1 sheet pros and cons on him as a man, 2nd sheet on your relationship and the 3rd on you leaving. You need to see your situation in black and* white to make a decision. Commit to your church for the next 30 days and let God show you signs on what to do.

DON'T - *Nag over and over. It is not fixing the problem. At this point, you need to reach down and get the courage to show you do not care. It is the only way the situation can turn around. The less you show you care, the more it will get his attention.*

While in a relationship, it is important to maintain your worth and keep his attention. Make sure daily you keep yourself together - hair, make-up and smelling good. Men notice when their woman falls off and starts not to care. When you stop caring about your personal appearance, his eyes might start wondering toward women who do care about their personal appearance. I am not saying that it's right, but your value should be shown daily.

DO - *Try on new dresses and outfits in front of him, get his opinion on what he likes and does not like. Remember, the only person you should be trying to impress is your man. Stop wearing the "granny panties" to bed all the time. Dress sexy every once and a while. Doll yourself up when you go out on dates, throw on some high hills and let your hair down. Show him every time you go out the house that you are still that woman he fell in love with.*

DON'T - *Ignore what he likes. What he likes keeps his attention. Men are very simple, so make sure you keep things simple. Listen and apply to his simple likes and your value will never go away.*

How to know when it's time to let go.

Some of the hardest things about your value and worth as a woman are maintaining it. Also remember, what you put up with, you end up with! If you find yourself doing nothing, but complaining you need to weigh your options of leaving. Happiness is more important than love. Everyone finds love, but everyone is not happy. You will have issues in your relationship that is a part of life. But these issues should not go on for weeks, months and years. Last, once you lost your value, you basically lost your respect and he will run over you as long as you let him. Always know your value and what you bring to the table, and he will know your worth.

If you need help with prayer, start with this prayer below.

Our Father in heaven,

hallowed be your name,

your kingdom come,

your will be done,

on earth as it is in heaven.

Give us today our daily bread.

And forgive us our debts,

as we also have forgiven our debtors.

And lead us not into temptation,

but deliver us from the evil one.

(Matthew 6: 10-13)

For relationship coaching or help with your concerns with your marriage and preparing yourself for a relationship, contact Coaching@TerryBams.com.

Add me on Facebook at

www.Facebook.com/AuthorTerryBams

Follow me on Twitter at

www.Twitter.com/MrBams

Check out my website at

www.TerryBams.com

For booking, contact me at

authorterrybams@gmail.com

CPSIA information can be obtained at www.ICGtesting.com
Printed in the USA
BVOW021857100613

322930BV00009B/165/P